MY GRANDMA AND ME

COLORING BOOK

by

PENELOPE ANNE COLE

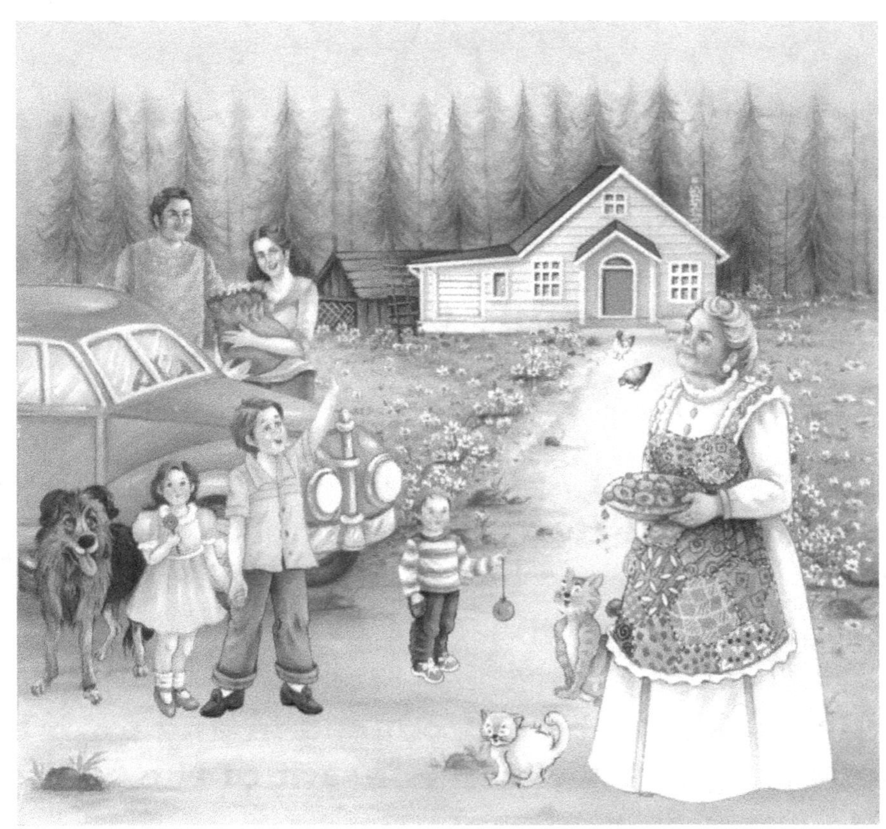

Illustrator Rama Dixit

Published by Magical Book Works

www.magicalbookworks.com

Dedication

To Grandmothers, Grandmas, Nanas,

and their beloved grandchildren

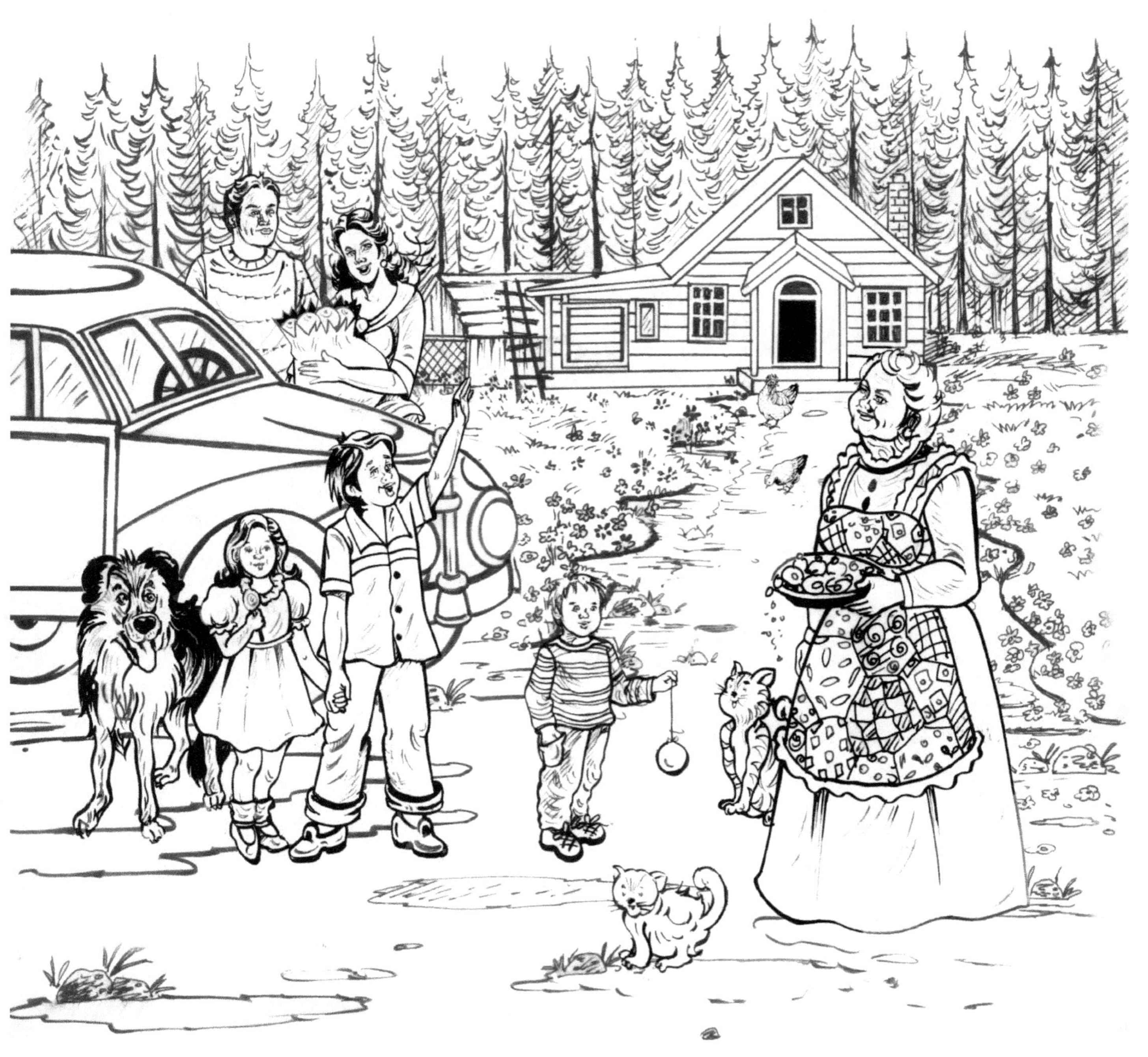

See us arrive at Grandma's house.
We're ready for some fun.

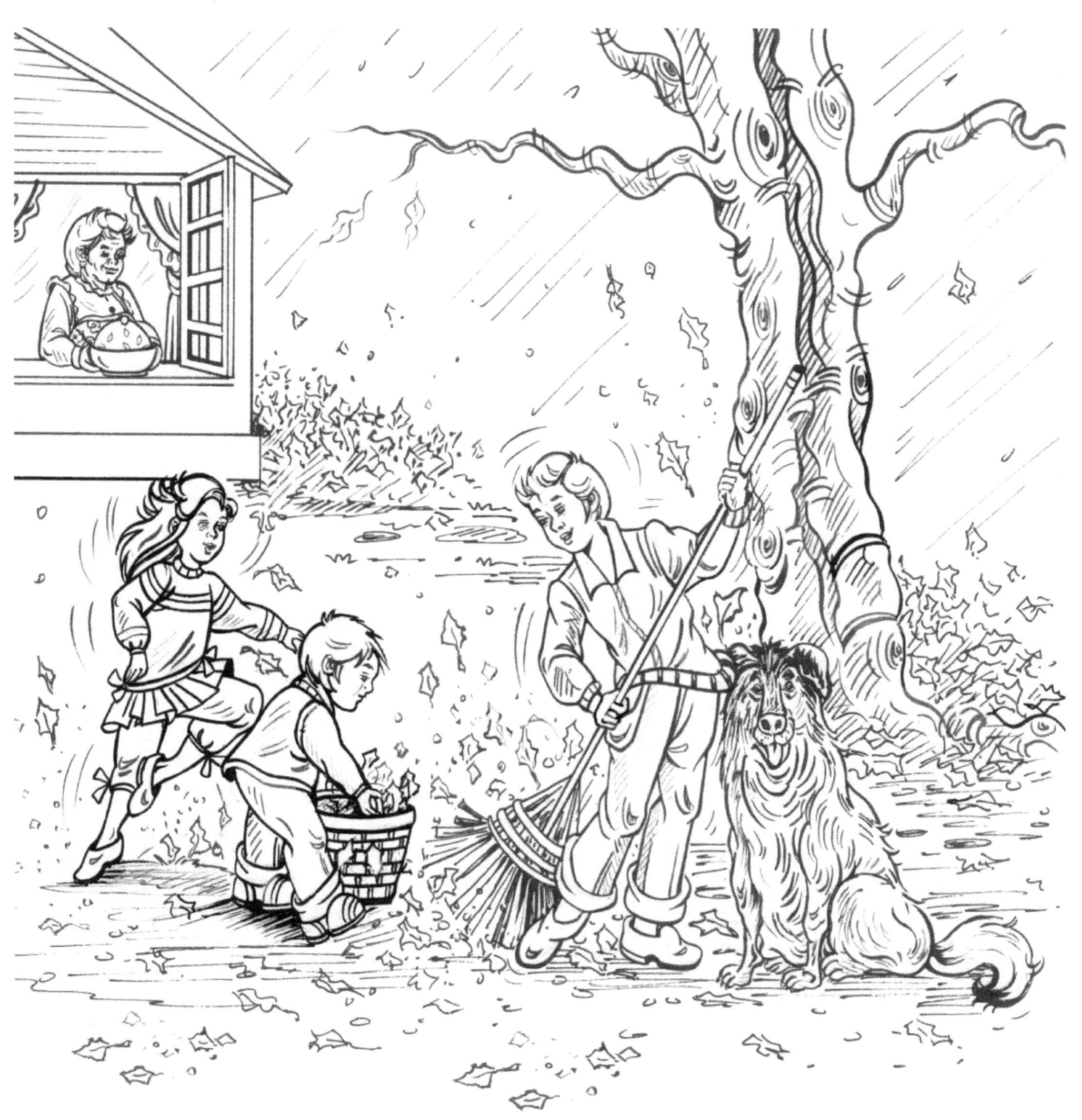

We'll help rake fallen leaves for her.
Nice treats when we are done.

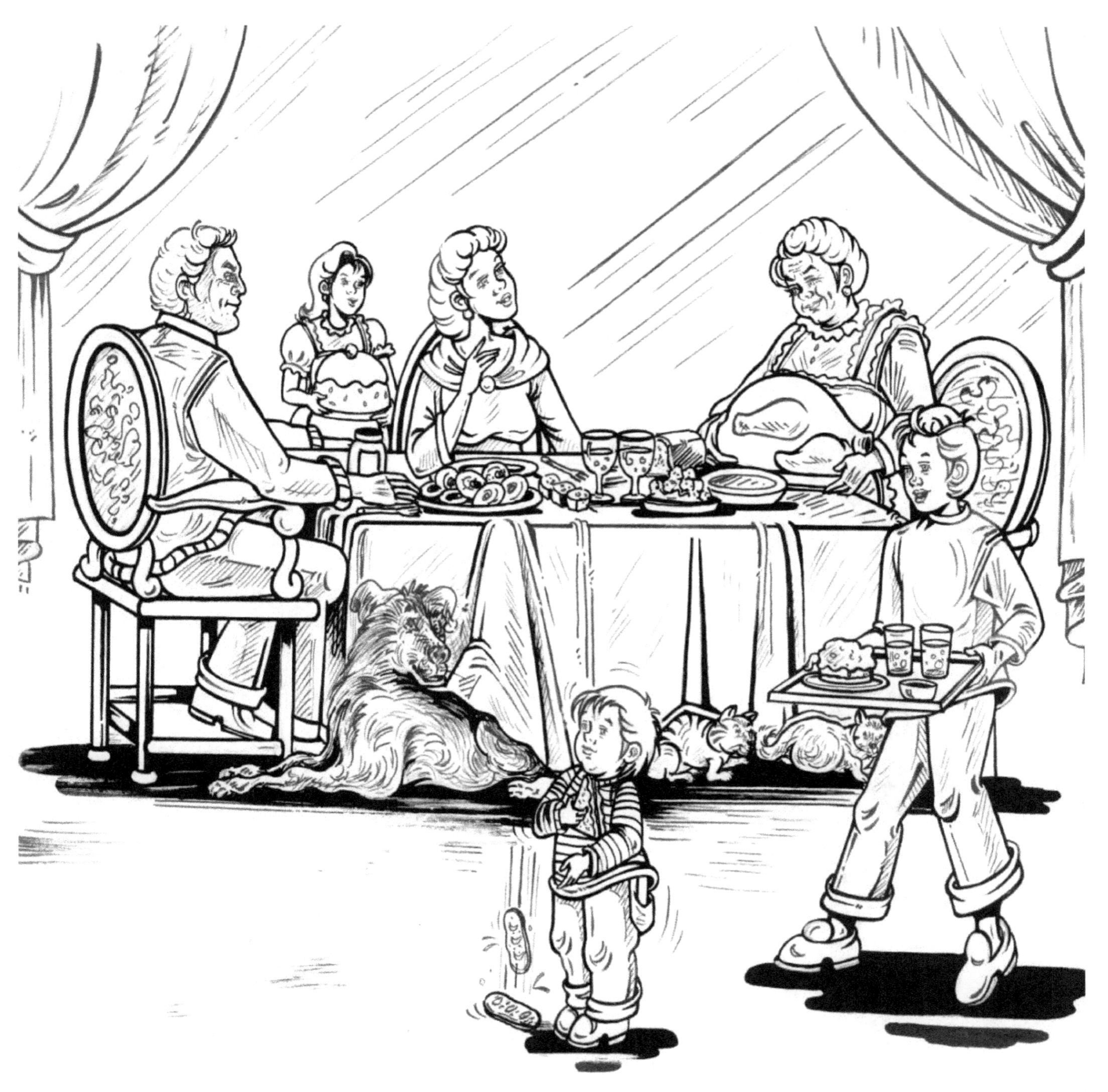

Thanksgiving's such a special day—
delicious food we eat.
We help Grandma prepare the feast—
with fun-filled games a treat.

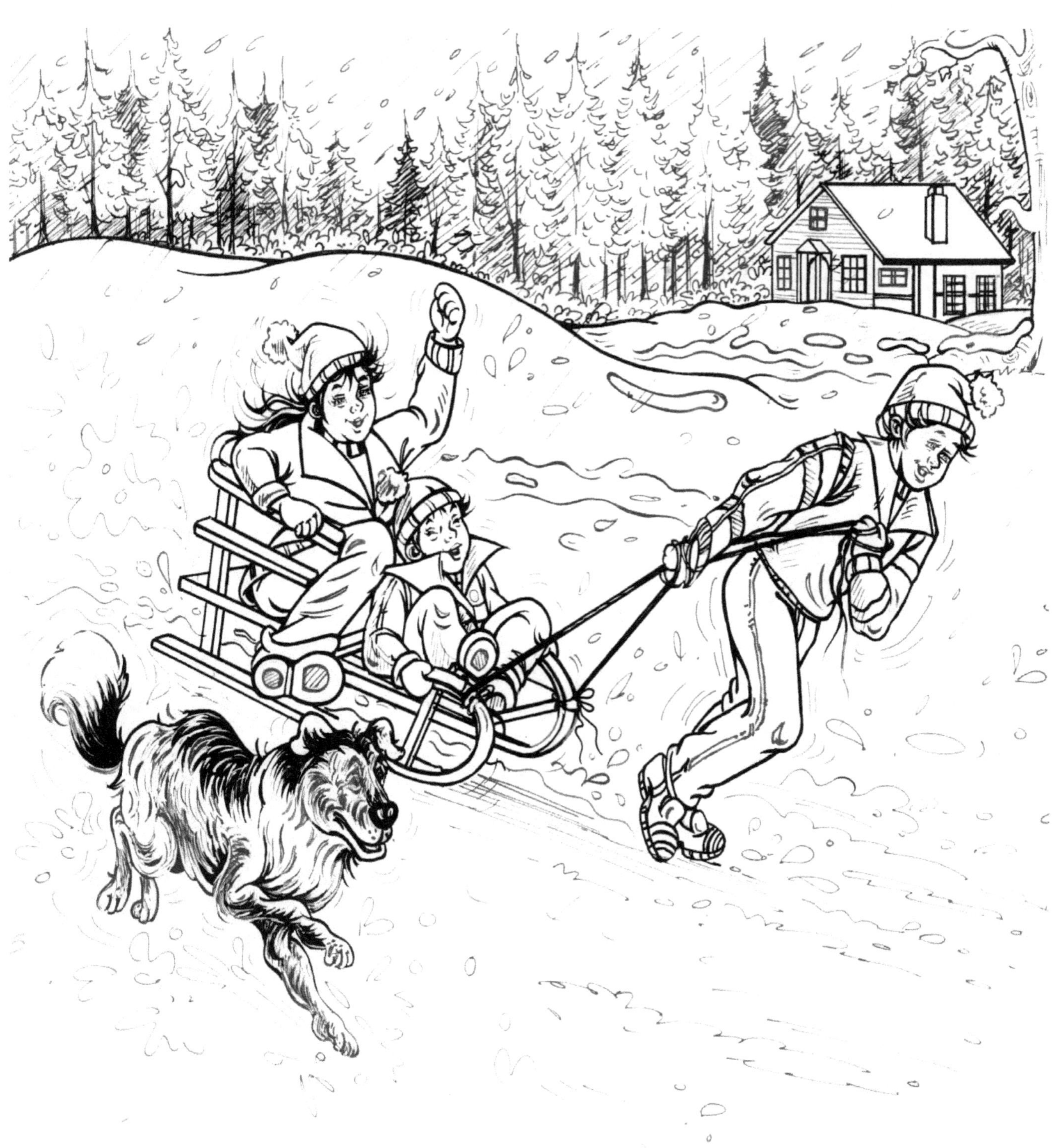

Then winter snow brings sledding time for happy girls and boys.

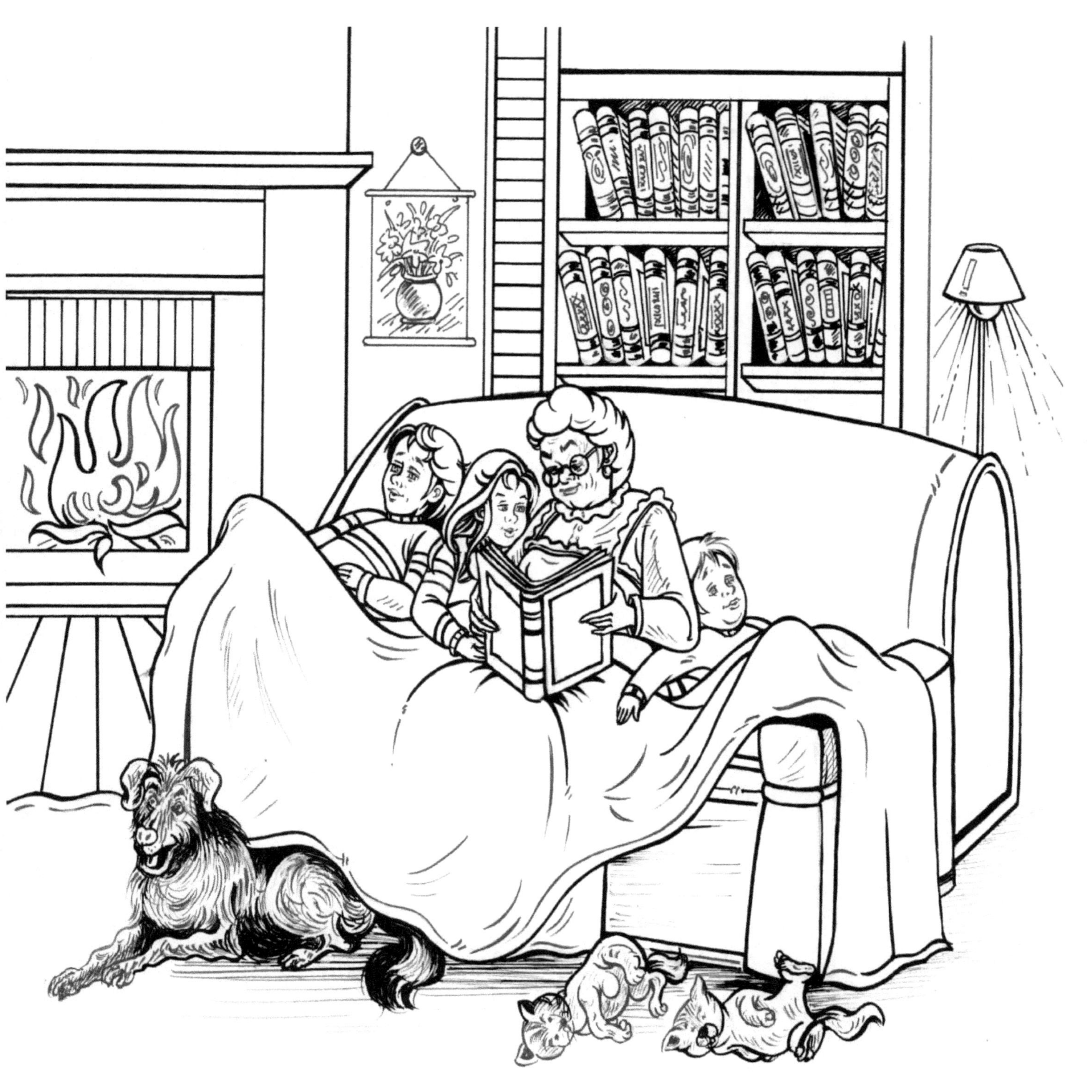

**Warm fire with Grandma reading books—
we like them more than toys.**

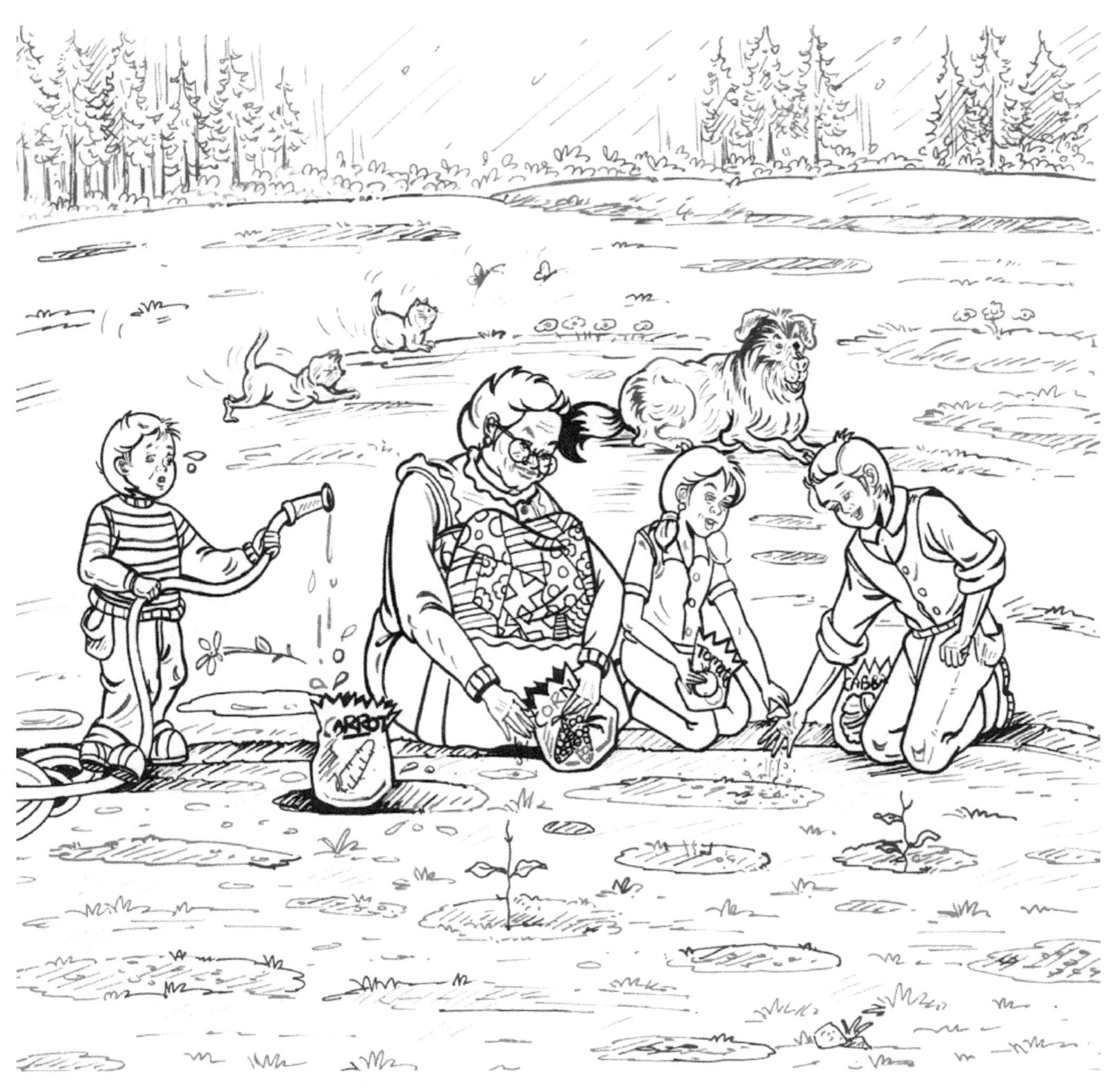

Spring brings new veggie seeds to plant.
We help her with this chore.
We see young plants push up new leaves.
We'll have fresh fruit and more.

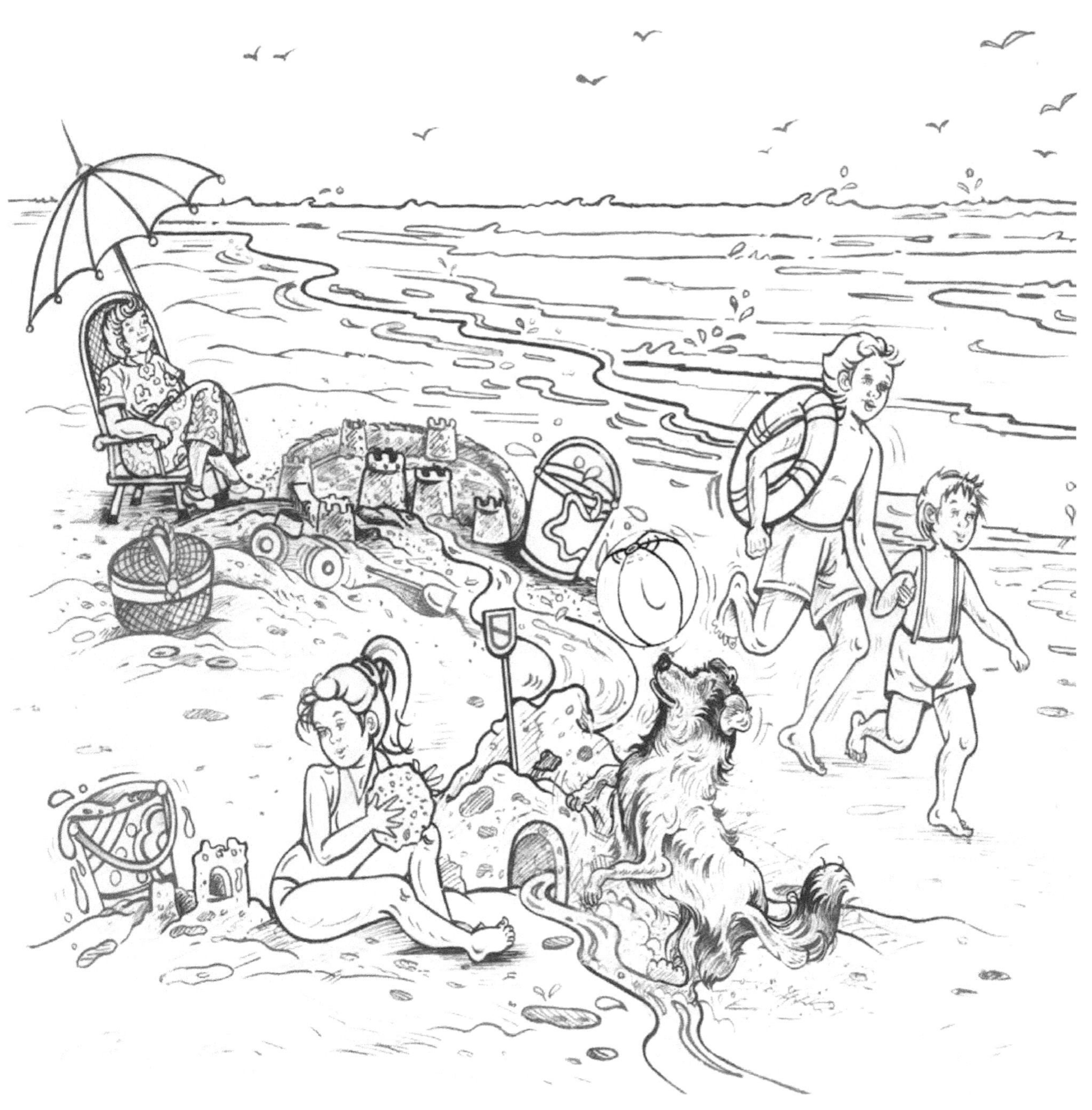

Our beach time play with Grandma near—
long summer days we share.
There's lots for us to eat and do
We're safe under her care.

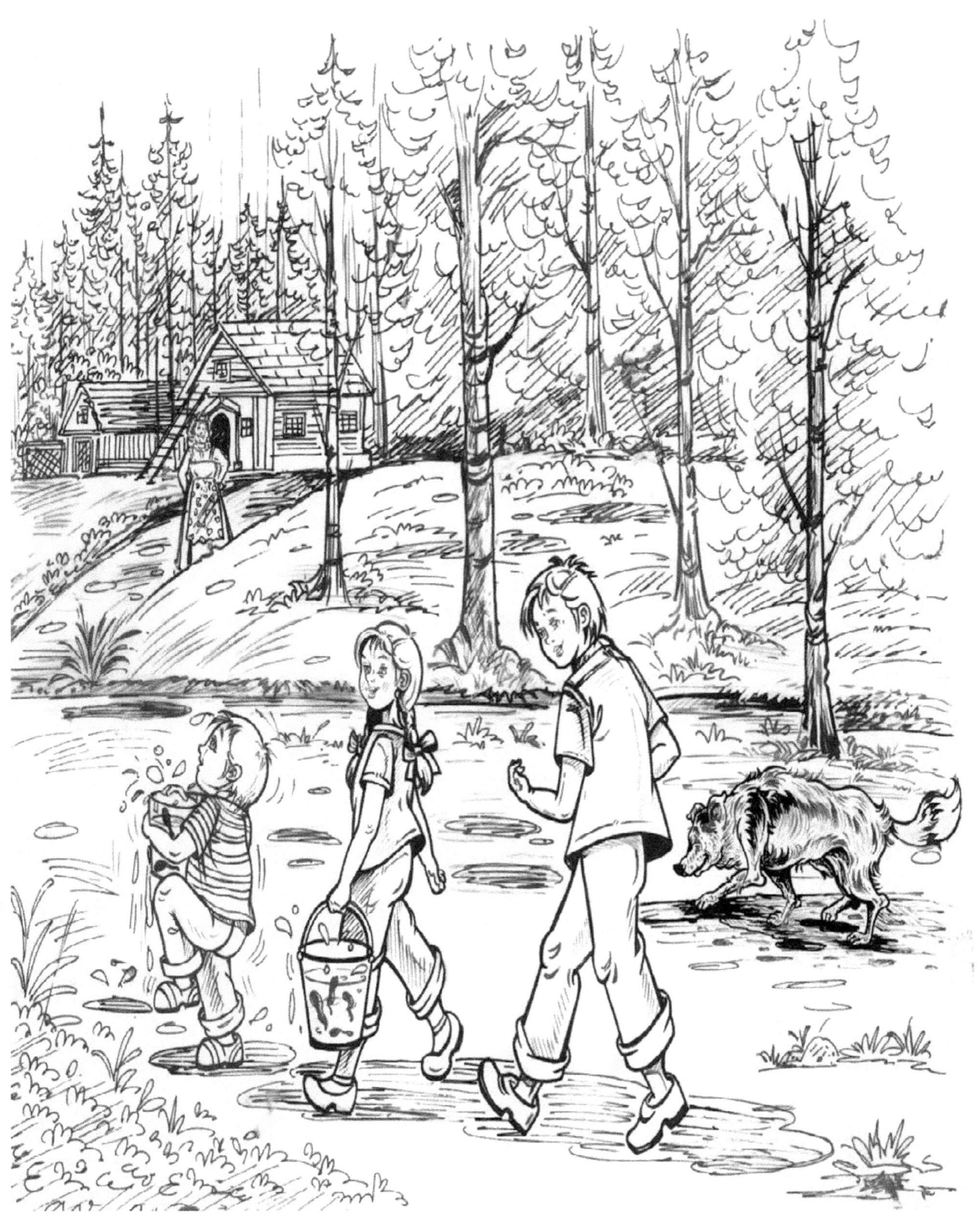

Our days are full with climbing trees, rescuing birds, and such.

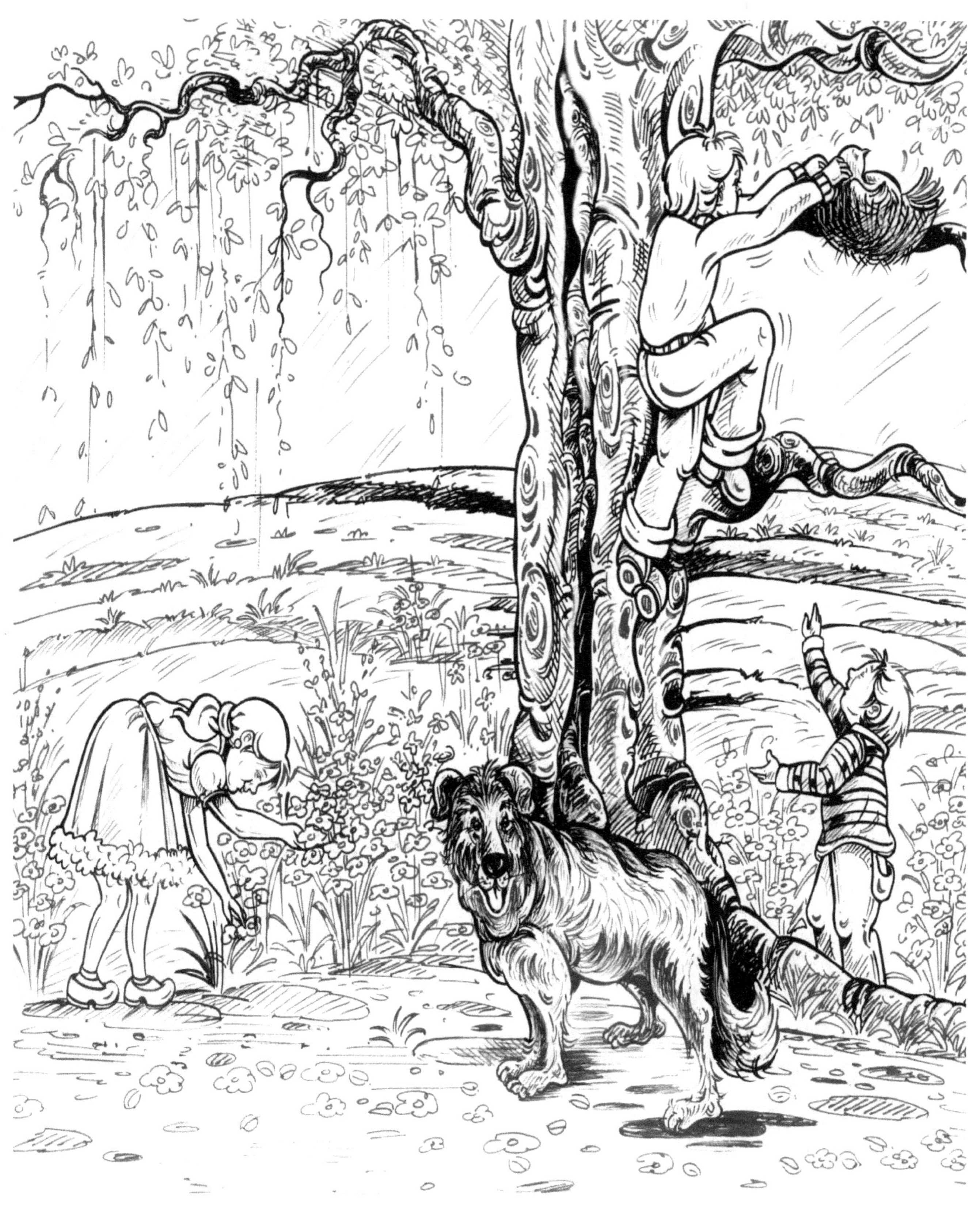

Pick up some wildflowers for Grandma, and other things we touch.

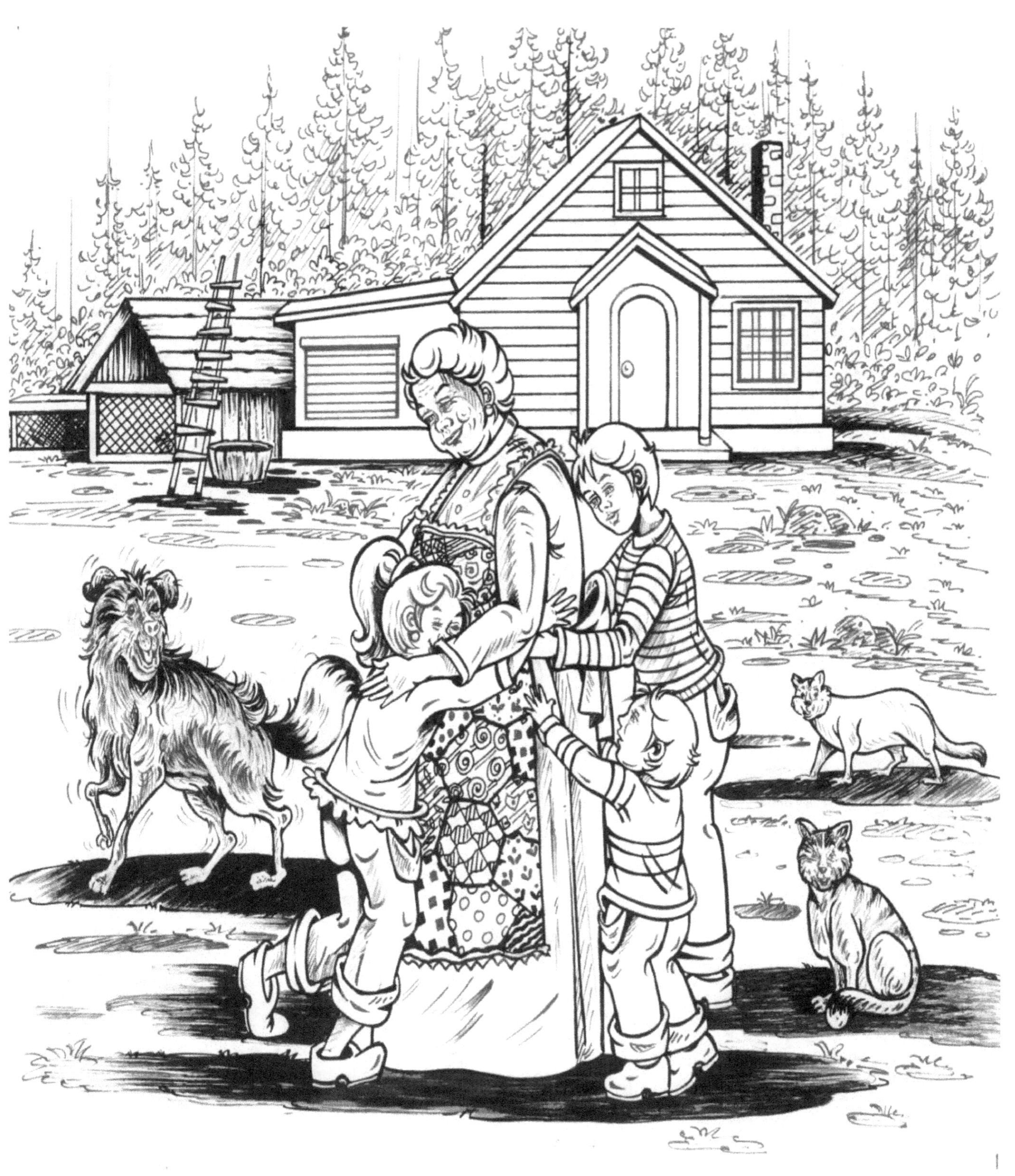

Grandma is there to give us hugs and chase away our fears.

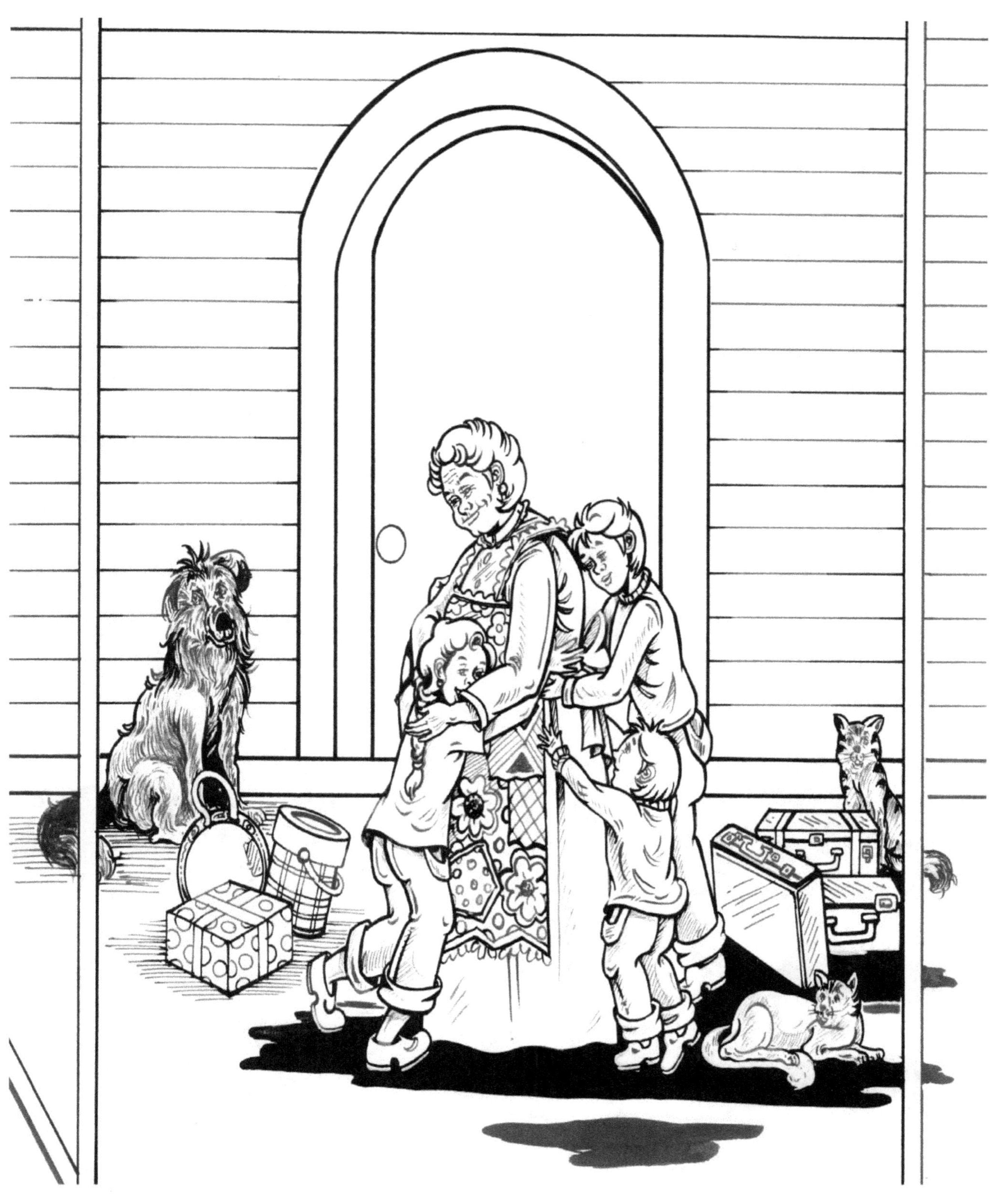

It's hard to leave when fall arrives.
She wipes away our tears.

Books in English by Penelope Anne Cole

The Magical Series:

Magical Matthew:
Matthew secretly fixes things by magic for his family and friends. Later he expands his good deeds. (1st in the Magical Series) Ages 5-8

Magical Mea:
Mea wants to test her magical ability. What can she do? What might happen to a little girl on the loose with magic? (2nd Magical book) Ages 5-8

Magical Mea Goes to School:
Mea's now in Second Grade. She wants more play time after school, but her big brother Matt wants her to practice using her magic secretly. (3rd Magical book) Ages 5-8

Magical Max and Magical Mickey:
College bound Matt, and middle school Mea, are surprised when Mom announces she's having twin boys. Everyone wonders if they be magical, too. (4th Magical book) Ages 5-8

Magical Max and Magical Mickey's Big Surprise:
Nine year old twins Max and Mickey know they'll soon lose their magic. They're working hard on a surprise graduation gift before their magic runs out. (5th Magical Book) Ages 5-8

*****

What's for Dinner?:
Katy is invited to her Nigerian friend Amaeka's for dinner and fears their food may be too strange and she might not like it. Ages 5-8

My Grandma's Pink House:
Remembrance of a simpler life and time—of children playing in the woods, at the beach, in the garden, helping and visiting Grandma in all seasons. Ages 5-8

My Grandma and Me Coloring Book:
A coloring book for children to remember special times spent with Grandma. Ages 5-8

In and Out, All 'Round About–Opposite Friends:
About two friends, who are different and pull in opposite directions, but are still friends. Ages 4-7

Ten Little Tricksters:
A reverse counting Halloween book shows little ghosts, goblins, monsters, ogres, bats, zombies, skeletons, witches, black cats, and a pumpkin all out trick or treating.. Pre-K, Kinder, 1st Grade

Libros en español

La serie mágica:

Mateo Mágico

Mía Mágica

Mía Mágica va a la escuela

Max Mágico y Miguel Mágico

Max Mágico y Miguel Mágico y la gran sorpresa

*****

¿Que vamos a comer?

*****

Para pre-kínder y kínder:
Diez pequeños bromistas

Magical BookWorks

www.magicalbookworks.com

Author

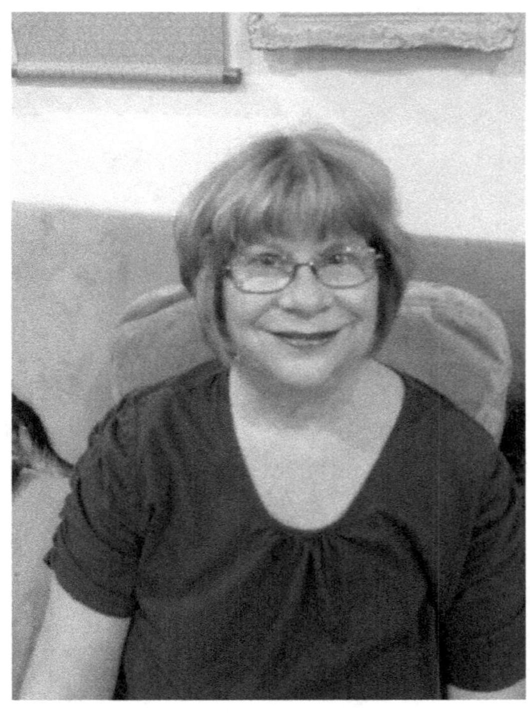

www.penelopeannecole.com

Penelope Anne Cole has taught and tutored at every grade level. She enjoys writing children's stories to be read aloud. "Reading to children is the best way to help them love literature." Check out her award winning Magical Series of books for ages 5 to 8: *Magical Matthew, Magical Mea, Magical Mea Goes to School, Magical Max* and *Magical Mickey, Magical Max and Magical Mickey's Big Surprise.*

When not writing or reviewing children's books, Ms. Cole tutors, enjoys dog walking, reading, gardening, church and choir. She is a member of the SCBWI, a member of the California Writers Club, and is a Reading Therapist with Read America.

Author

[illegible]

Penelope [illegible] has taught and tutored at every grade level. She enjoys writing children's stories to be read aloud. "Reading to children is the best way to help them love life and [illegible]" [illegible] award-winning "Magical" Series of books [illegible] *Magical* [illegible] *Magical* [illegible] *Magical* [illegible] and [illegible] *Magical Mommy* [illegible] Michael's Big Surprise.

When [illegible] children's [illegible] a [illegible] gardening, [illegible] She is a member of [illegible] a member of the California Writers Club and is [illegible] with [illegible]

Illustrator

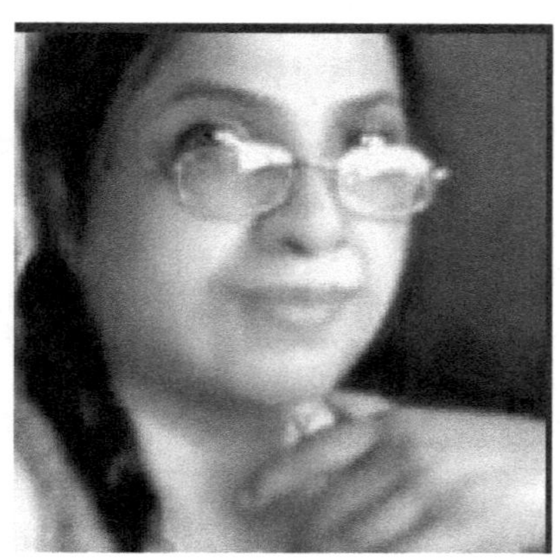

Rama Dixit is a self-taught illustrator with no art school experience. She's been an artist since her childhood. Her mentor, Mr. D.H. Kunte, taught her how to paint. Ms. Dixit also belongs to a very creative family. Her father, Professor C.K. Dixit, is a Poet, Writer, and Head of the Department at Mumbai University. Her mother is also a very good artist. Ms. Dixit was inspired by both of her parents to pursue a career as an artist.

Ms. Dixit's initial works were for greeting cards, pharmaceutical visual aids, and other stationery design work. Still those were not enough. She wanted to do more creative work and expand into other artwork. Ms. Dixit made a conscious effort to specialize in children's artwork. She believes that illustrating children's emotions is a big challenge. She believes that your ability to create effectively increases your ability to capture the images you visualize. Technique and creativity go hand in hand!

www.ingramcontent.com/pod-product-compliance
Lightning Source LLC
LaVergne TN
LVHW080329110826
845155LV00026B/232

* 9 7 8 1 9 4 3 1 9 6 1 0 4 *